I'M GOOD AT
MEDIA
WHAT JOB CAN I GET?

Richard Spilsbury

WAYLAND

First published in 2013 by Wayland
Copyright Wayland 2013

Wayland
Hachette Children's Books
338 Euston Road
London NW1 3BH

Wayland Australia
Level 17/207 Kent Street,
Sydney, NSW 2000

Commissioning editor: Victoria Brooker
Project editor: Kay Barnham
Designer: Tim Mayer
Picture research: Richard Spilsbury
Proofreader: Alice Harman

Produced for Wayland by
White-Thomson Publishing Ltd
www.wtpub.co.uk
+44 (0)843 2087 460

British Library Cataloguing in Publication Data

Spilsbury, Richard, 1963-
I'm good at media - what job can I get?.
1. Mass media–Vocational guidance–Juvenile
literature.
I. Title
302.2'3'023-dc23

ISBN-13: 9780750277679

Printed in China

Wayland is a division of Hachette Children's Books
an Hachette UK company
www.hachette.co.uk

Picture credits

1. Shutterstock/Songquan Deng; 3. Shutterstock/Maxisport; 4. Dreamstime/Artofchriz; 5. Dreamstime/Gan Hui; 6. Shutterstock/IvicaNS; 7. Shutterstock/IvicaNS; 8. Dreamstime/Hupeng; 9. Dreamstime/Alexander Kirch; 10. Dreamstime/Edward Fielding; 11. Dreamstime/Denis Makarenko; 12. Shutterstock/Rob Kemp ; 13. Dreamstime/Alexander Podshivalov; 14. Shutterstock/Songquan Deng; 15. Dreamstime/Yuri Arcurs; 16. Shutterstock/Tsian; 17. Shutterstock/Maxisport; 18. Shutterstock/Darren Brode; 19. Shutterstock/Adriano Castelli; 20. Shutterstock/Terry Straehley; 21. Dreamstime/Andrei Calangiu; 22. Dreamstime/Imagesolution; 23. Shutterstock/Yuri Arcurs; 24. Shutterstock/mashurov; 25. Dreamstime/Araraadt; 26. Shutterstock/Florian ISPAS; 27. Shutterstock/andrea michele piacquadio; 28. Dreamstime/Hongqi Zhang; 29. Shutterstock/Sylvie Bouchar; cover (top left), Shutterstock/IvicaNS; cover (top right), Shutterstock/Songquan Deng; cover (bottom), Shutterstock/Tsian.

Disclaimer

The website addresses (URLs) included in this book were valid at the time of going to press. However, because of the nature of the Internet, it is possible that some addresses may have changed, or sites may have changed or closed down since publication. While the author and Publisher regret any inconvenience this may cause the readers, no responsibility for any such changes can be accepted by either the author or Publisher.

CONTENTS

The world of media   4

Programme researcher   6

Media planner   8

Runner   10

TV producer-director   12

Advertising account executive   14

Broadcast journalist   16

Information officer   18

Screenwriter   20

Magazine features editor   22

Assistant film editor   24

TV presenter   26

Social media strategist   28

Glossary   30

Further information   31

Index   32

The world of media

Switch on the TV, open a magazine or turn on your mobile and you have instant access to information and entertainment. You can see adverts for a wide range of products, from sweets to dental floss, and also details of programmes, films, charity campaigns and events to see. Media is all about communicating and media industries rely on methods such as TV, radio, cinema, newspapers, Internet sites and billboard posters to do this.

PROFESSIONAL VIEWPOINT

'Media has a knack of attracting great people. So whether you're planning, persuading, generating ideas, explaining, collaborating, buying, selling or socialising, people who think fast, communicate clearly and can have some fun along the way tend to do well in this business.'

Jeremy Tester, Director of Insight, Sky Media

↑ Using media – such as adverts and TV broadcasts or podcasts of concerts and interviews – can help propel a locally successful musician such as Jay Z to global superstardom.

The importance of media

Media spreads ideas and culture amongst people. When Martin Luther nailed his new religious ideas to a church door for people to read in 1517, it led to major changes in churches in Europe. In 2011, social media spread revolution across North Africa and the Middle East. The media has encouraged people to change their lifestyles in recent decades, for example from landlines to mobiles, from local trips to foreign holidays and from letters to emails.

↑ New technology – such as Apple's iPad – is yet another way for people to access the media.

Media industries

The major media industries include advertising, film, TV, radio, publishing, marketing, and interactive media from video games to social networking sites. Their success relies on reaching people who may be persuaded, by what the industries communicate, to buy a new product or a ticket for a film, give to a charity or join a social movement for change. Media industries are major employers in many countries. Around half a million people work in media in the UK alone.

Special skills

To work in the fascinating world of media, you need good communication skills – both verbal and written. You should also be able to find the best ways of spreading information and have the ability to criticise and analyse ideas. An interest in keeping up to date with changes in technology that could affect media is essential. If you have these skills, or would like to develop them, then working in media could be just right for you!

Programme researcher

Programme researchers look for and find the information, locations and people that help to bring TV and radio programmes to life. They often work on a range of different aspects of a programme. They collect and check that facts used in a programme are accurate, contact people to be interviewed, find and price locations for a programme to be filmed in, look for video clips to be used in a documentary and write briefs for presenters.

↑ Part of a programme researcher's job might involve finding their way around archives and libraries to find information for programmes.

What skills do I need?

Programme researchers need to be very organised to keep track of facts, figures and contact details. They also need good communication skills to phone and interview a wide range of people. Accuracy and an ability to write clearly are vital when presenting information to presenters and producers. Most programme researchers have a degree, for example in media studies, journalism or English, and/or a postgraduate journalism qualification.

PROFESSIONAL VIEWPOINT

'I find it really helpful for the producers if you condense all that [research] into the most salient points. So, who the main contacts are, the logistics of filming – what time of year, what the main story is and why or where it fits in the grand scheme of the programme.'
Sophie Lanfear, BBC Natural History Unit researcher

Programme researchers do a lot of the research that's used by presenters when interviewing people.

Different types of programme researcher

A researcher might work on a wide variety of programmes or specialise in a particular area, such as history or wildlife programmes. If you specialise, the work you do depends on the area you choose. For example, a researcher on natural history programmes will read and research scientific papers and interview scientists and then summarise facts from this research in their briefs for producers. A researcher on history documentaries will spend more time checking archives for film, video and photographic material.

Job description

Programme researchers:
• gather and present information, facts and figures
• source contacts and arrange interviews and meetings with relevant people
• research archives for music, stills and other footage
• obtain permission for the use of copyrighted material such as music and video footage
• write briefing notes and scripts for producers and presenters
• organise locations, equipment hire and freelance staff
• prepare cost accounts.

Media planner

Have you ever noticed how adverts for energy drinks are shown in the half-time break in a TV football match or how holiday adverts appear in the travel pages of a newspaper? A media planner makes sure that advertising campaigns are seen by as many of their target audience as possible. They analyse who uses and watches different media and entertainment, from magazines to social media websites. Then they choose which is going to be the most effective place, time or format to reach them.

Media planners pick the best places to show ads so that a product gets noticed.

_ Job description

Media planners:

- work with the client and the account team to understand the client's advertising needs
- research and interpret statistics about the target audience's media habits
- plan the best times, locations and forms of media to show campaigns
- present proposals, schedules and costs to clients
- work closely with creative teams, researchers and other members of the advertising team
- work with a media buyer to cost and book advertising space
- build relationships with managers of newspapers, magazines and websites.

What skills do I need?

You need good research skills, so you can compare and analyse advertising statistics and strategies. You should also have strong presentation and negotiation skills, and an understanding of business and the media. It helps if you can think creatively about what might catch consumers' interest. Most media planners have degrees or HNDs, often in subjects such as media studies, business management, marketing or advertising.

PROFESSIONAL VIEWPOINT
'It's definitely fun to work on campaigns from start to finish and see everything come to life, but I really like the psychological aspect of media planning. There's more to it than people realise, because you really have to dive into consumer behaviour and understand who your target is, how they think, and what they do.'
Jessica, digital media planner

Different types of media planner

Larger advertising and media agencies usually have separate media planners and media buyers, but some may combine these jobs. This means that as well as planning, the job would include negotiating and buying media space at the best rates, researching and booking slots that reach the widest target audience, managing budgets and monitoring the effectiveness of campaigns.

➡ Digital media planning is an area that is growing rapidly. It includes social media such as Twitter and Facebook.

Runner

→ Being a runner allows to you to learn what goes on behind the scenes during the production process of a film or TV programme.

In the film and TV industries, a runner is not a sprinter or a hurdler! They are general assistants who work behind the scenes in the production department. Runners do small but essential jobs in the production office and on locations. As the name suggests, their main job is to 'run' errands, carrying drinks, messages and scripts to where they are needed. But they do other things too, from cleaning-up a film set after a shoot to meeting and greeting important guests and film and TV stars.

Job description

Runners:
- collect and deliver equipment, scripts and other items
- distribute messages and post
- do filing and photocopying and answer the phone
- transport cast, crew and production staff between offices, studios and locations
- find props
- greet and look after visitors and studio guests
- keep sets clean and tidy
- make and hand out tea, coffee and lunches.

Runners can work in any area of film or TV production, including the production office, on set, in art departments or animation studios and in post-production offices. Being a runner is a great way to break into the TV and film industries. You gain experience and understanding of what's involved in the production process, and build up contacts who might offer you a job later.

What skills do I need?

You don't need to be a graduate to be a runner, but an HND, degree or other qualification in film, TV or media might increase your chances. Experience is important, so take any chance you have to work on school or campus newspapers, or on local radio or TV stations. You need to be good with people, hard-working, enthusiastic and willing to take on any task. You also need to show initiative, for example knowing where to find a missing prop, fast!

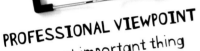
PROFESSIONAL VIEWPOINT

'The most important thing I found to do is to keep smiling... Try and make as many contacts with as many people in different departments as possible, whether it be a producer who you hope will one day give you a job, or the cleaners who if onside will come and empty the bin bags in one of the client areas quicker.'
Louise McNamara, ex-runner

➡ Successful film director Quentin Tarantino started out as a runner at a film studio.

TV producer-director

TV producer-directors are responsible for getting TV programmes or films out on time, to budget and to the highest quality. A producer-director chooses what to include in a show and creates its whole mood, from the way it looks to the background music.

➜

TV producer-directors are responsible for everything in a programme, from finding the perfect location to directing the film crew and actors.

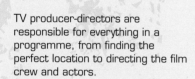

Job description

TV producer-directors:
- research and choose stories and features for films and programmes
- commission writers and assess and edit ideas and scripts
- create the mood and look of a film, for example by choosing locations and sound effects
- brief assistant producers and researchers
- brief and work with presenters and actors
- direct the film crew
- organise shooting schedules
- manage every aspect of production to meet deadlines
- ensure programmes are the best they can be for the allotted budget.

Usually, a broadcaster comes up with the basic outline for a one-off show or series. Then it is the producer-director's job to choose the words and pictures that will tell that story. They lead a team of people, including an editor and a film crew, to help them research, write, direct and edit the programme. Together they make the programme into something that can be clearly understood and appreciated by a wide audience.

What skills do I need?

TV producer-directors need to communicate ideas and information clearly and concisely, not only to the teams who work for them but also to the viewers. They need a wide knowledge and experience of television production processes such as lighting, sound, camera and editing equipment and techniques. They also need to be able to write well so they can edit or help to produce scripts and voiceovers. Most TV producer-directors study for a degree and then get work experience before training on the job as an assistant producer.

When shooting is over, TV producer-directors oversee the editing process that reduces hours and hours of filming down to a finished programme.

Advertising account executive

Think of the simple, clear adverts for Apple products. They are the product of negotiations between Apple, which wants to sell its products to a wide audience, and an advertising company, which wants to help them do this by highlighting the high-tech features and design that make people want to buy iPads, iPhones and other Apple products. An advertising account executive acts as the link between an advertising agency and its clients.

PROFESSIONAL VIEWPOINT

'This job is suited to someone who likes a challenge, and who is prepared to put in long hours when required. You must pay attention to detail and have wonderful communication skills, as a third of your day is spent talking to your client.'

Kate, advertising account executive

For many account executives, seeing the advertisements they helped to put together in magazines, on TV or on the street is their favourite part of the job.

What skills do I need?

All advertising account executives need great communication and presentation skills, as well as the ability to negotiate, for example, to ask copywriters to revise campaign ideas according to clients' wishes. Unless they can deliver the campaigns a client wants, the client may take their business to another advertising agency! It is best to gain work experience in an advertising agency before looking for your first job, and it may help if you have a BTEC, HND or degree in a subject such as media studies, advertising, marketing, business or management.

An advertising account executive first learns what their client wants to sell. Then they work with their agency's copywriters (who come up with the words) and illustrators/photographers (who come up with the images) to develop effective advertising campaigns that meet the client's approval.

Advertising account executives spend a lot of time talking to their clients. →

Job description

Advertising account executives:
- meet clients to discuss their advertising needs
- work with a team of staff to ensure the campaign they design meets the client's brief
- present campaign ideas and costs to clients
- brief the creative team that produces the words and artwork
- negotiate with clients, solve problems and make sure that deadlines are met
- check the campaign's progress and ensure it stays on schedule and budget
- keep the client informed at all stages of the campaign
- try to win new business for the agency.

Broadcast journalist

↑ Preparing a broadcast involves taking large amounts of often complex information and presenting it in ways that people can understand and relate to.

A news anchor breaks a story about a natural disaster. A radio presenter interviews a politician in a programme that's investigating government corruption. These are both examples of broadcast journalists. They are people who present information about events or issues that affect people. They carefully research the information they receive and find out if it is true by consulting different sources. The best broadcasters present this information in an unbiased way to the public, who can then make up their own minds about its content.

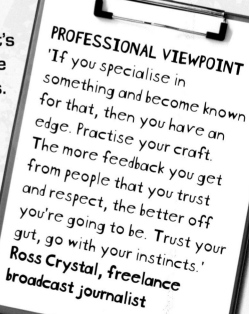

PROFESSIONAL VIEWPOINT
'If you specialise in something and become known for that, then you have an edge. Practise your craft. The more feedback you get from people that you trust and respect, the better off you're going to be. Trust your gut, go with your instincts.'
Ross Crystal, freelance broadcast journalist

Different types of broadcast journalist

Some broadcast journalists work for single television stations or newspapers, but others are freelancers who carry out projects for different clients. They work in all types of media from TV to the Internet and their work can be international or local. Some specialise in topics they have background knowledge of, such as law or the armed forces, but others may work on a range of subjects.

What skills do I need?

Broadcast journalists work day or night, depending when an event happens, to tight deadlines. It's their job to gather relevant information for a broadcast and they need to be self-motivated to follow through an idea to a finished broadcast. They can put interviewees at ease to get good broadcast material, ask probing yet sensitive questions and listen well. Most have a degree, sometimes in media and sometimes in broadcast journalism. Some move into this role after gaining experience working for newspapers.

Job description

Broadcast journalists:

- generate ideas and outlines for features, articles or broadcasts
- assemble information from many sources including press cuttings, interviews and books
- conduct interviews on camera and suggest additional recorded material to go in the broadcast to bring the story alive
- assist in editing recorded interviews and other material while assembling broadcasts
- prepare broadcasts on time and within budget.

← Broadcast journalists may have to adapt the content of their presentations on the spot. In sport, for example, when a game starts the journalist has no idea who will win!

Information officer

If you want to know about a nuclear power station, a forthcoming gallery exhibition or what a charity does, you might get in touch with their information officer. Information officers are the people who gather, analyse and communicate information about organisations or clients to the public. They may also be called press officers or press and media-relations officers.

PROFESSIONAL VIEWPOINT
'I think it's really important to get experience, even if it's only a couple of days working in a press office. This will really help when it comes to applying for jobs and show that you're committed to a career in the sector. You also need to be enthusiastic about what you're doing and willing to get stuck in!'
Kim Edward, press officer at Cancer Research UK

← Some information officers travel to trade fairs to help promote their company's products.

What skills do I need?

Information officers need to be very organised, with good IT skills that enable them to find, store and distribute information accurately. A major part of the job is meeting and getting to know people, so communication skills are essential. Most have a degree, often followed by a postgraduate course in this type of work.

Information officers find and store information, and then distribute it to the right people. For example, a theatre company's information officer collects and stores photos of shows on a database and uses these in press releases sent to journalists. Many information officers liaise with the media, organising meetings and developing press contacts that will be useful for their company.

Job description

Information officers:

- evaluate, classify and store information
- handle enquiries
- manage electronic information such as intranets or wikis
- develop new information systems
- develop media contacts
- write and edit information for factsheets, press releases and web pages
- attend press conferences and media interviews
- advertise, monitor and maintain the information service and media coverage.

Different types of information officer

Information officers work in many media industries such as TV and advertising. They also work in a wide range of companies or institutions, from government departments and museums, to private companies such as clothes manufacturers and also charities. Most information officers work for one company or a group of companies, although freelance work is possible.

↓ Information officers make sure that events like this photography exhibition attract crowds by distributing information about them to various media, including newspapers and online events guides.

Screenwriter

A screenwriter is involved with every story you watch on a screen, from a blockbuster film to a TV soap opera! They write scripts detailing the words spoken by characters, their actions and the settings where the story takes place.

Screenwriters come up with original stories and research them, for example, to make sure words and objects are accurate for the time and place in which the story is set. They adapt books and other material into scripts, too.

↑ Mark Fergus and Hawk Ostby are American screenwriters best known for their work on films such as *Iron Man* (2008).

Job description

Screenwriters:
- come up with themes and ideas
- prepare a pitch (short summary) of their ideas and present it to producers
- meet with producers to be briefed about a script idea the producer has developed
- research background information for the script
- write the script, develop plots and characters
- rewrite the script in line with producer's, script reader's and editor's suggestions, often over and over again.

Different types of screenwriter

Screenwriters write scripts for feature films, TV comedies and dramas, animation, children's programmes and computer games. They often specialise in a particular genre, or style, of writing such as historical or crime. Screenwriters are usually freelancers. They may write a script in the hope that a film or TV production company produces it, or they may be commissioned to write a script.

→ Screenwriters may spend a lot of time working alone so have to be able to motivate themselves to keep going.

PROFESSIONAL VIEWPOINT

'The best way to prepare yourself is to WRITE. Write every day. Whether it's a one-page skit, or The Great American Novel, the more you do it, the better you get... When you're not writing, STUDY. Read scripts. Watch your favourite movies and TV shows over and over again to learn their structure and style.'

Stephen Scaia, television and film screenwriter

What skills do I need?

A screenwriter has to be able to tell stories effectively for the screen – if dialogue is not interesting enough, viewers will shuffle around on their seats! Many great ideas are never made into films for many reasons, so screenwriters need to be able to cope with rejection and remain enthusiastic. These key skills are most important, but some screenwriters also have qualifications in media, creative writing, English or journalism.

Magazine features editor

Leaf through a magazine and your attention may be grabbed by an interview with your favourite film star, enticing places to go on holiday in Europe or what to wear this season. Magazine features editors are in charge of the main articles and reports published in magazines and online publications.

Features editors make sure their magazine is full of entertaining, high-quality, informative and interesting articles and images. They come up with ideas for features, commission work by writers and photographers or picture researchers, edit and proofread text, check layouts and manage an editorial team.

Readers might buy a magazine on impulse just because a great feature has grabbed their attention.

Job description

Magazine features editors:

- organise and chair editorial meetings
- work with writing staff to come up with ideas for articles and features
- commission articles from freelance and in-house writers
- read, write and research features and articles
- decide which features will appear in which issue
- rewrite, edit and proofread articles, returning some for revision
- meet with writers and artists to oversee design, artwork, layout and features
- choose photos and oversee photoshoots
- attend relevant events, fairs and conferences.

What skills do I need?

Magazine features editors need to be able to organise and manage a team of people, giving criticism and feedback, while keeping them motivated and working to deadlines. Magazines are regular publications that have to be ready on time. Most features editors have a degree in subjects such as media studies, English or journalism, but specialist magazines often require a degree in a relevant subject.

↓ Magazine features editors try to pick the best images to go with each article.

Different types of magazine features editor

The type of features an editor works on depends on the magazine. A food magazine might have a feature on olive oil, while a computer magazine has a feature on new software. Some features editors work on magazines for the general public, but others may have specialist knowledge to work on publications for specialist audiences, such as medical journals.

Assistant film editor

Feature films such as the *Lord of the Rings* trilogy are exciting experiences for the audience. This is partly because of the script and the actors, but also because of the way different action sequences, music and sound effects are blended together. The people partly responsible for that blend are assistant film editors.

↑ Assistant film editors work on special equipment in editing suites.

Job description

Assistant film editors:

• work with the editor and director to maximise the potential of the screenplay in choosing how sequences are filmed and put together
• cut down film sequences into shorter segments and order them into scenes
• adjust the content and pace of scenes so that they fit well together into a whole film
• add sound effects and music to fit the visuals, increasing their impact.

Different types of editor

Assistant film editors work for the editor, who usually has more experience. The editing team starts with many hours of action, close-ups, scenery and dialogue produced by the director. Their first edit pieces together film sequences and is roughly complete. It is then checked and adjusted by the editor, director and producer of the film before a final edit is ready to be shown in cinemas. Most editors are freelancers employed on a film-by-film basis.

What skills do I need?

Assistant film editors need a strong sense of how a film story unfolds, because scenes are not always shot in order. They need great patience and IT skills as they may work long hours using complex computer equipment. Many assistant film editors have taken courses in film editing at college or university, and have often worked for several years as trainees in TV companies before moving into film. It really helps to gain early experience, perhaps directing a play at college or making your own short films at home or in a school film club.

PROFESSIONAL VIEWPOINT

'Film editing is why people like movies. Because, in the end, wouldn't we all want to edit our own lives? I think everybody would like to take out the bad parts, take out the slow parts and look deeper into the good parts.'

Rob Cohen, film editor

↑ Editors pull together recorded material from different sources and put it together into finished films.

TV presenter

Presenters such as Ant and Dec, Dermot O'Leary and Lauren Laverne represent the face and the personality of a television show. Their job is to entertain and inform audiences on national and regional television, and satellite and cable channels.

Even though TV presenters usually follow a script during live broadcasts, they may have to 'ad lib' (react quickly to unplanned events) at times.

Different types of TV presenter

TV presenters work on live or recorded programmes, from shopping channels to chat shows or children's programmes. Some presenters are experts in the subject matter of the programme they present, such as sport or history, but others are employed because of their personality, character or TV experience. TV presenters are usually freelancers hired for particular shows, but may be contracted to work for particular TV companies or channels.

What skills do I need?

What would you do if you were presenting a chat show and a guest walked out or your microphone failed? A presenter needs to be able to handle unexpected events when necessary. They also need a good speaking voice and a memory for facts or storylines. Although there are no set entry qualifications, a degree in communication or media studies may be helpful. Many presenters start out as journalists or researchers, or in entertainment such as acting or comedy.

TV presenters:

- meet with the production team to go through the running order of the show
- rehearse and sometimes prepare their scripts
- present shows, for example by reading from an autocue or interviewing guests
- go through several 'takes' if necessary
- react to instructions given through an earpiece by the director or floor manager.

TV presenters introduce guests and themes, host a show, take part in the show's activities or narrate what happens or what is shown. A good presenter engages with the viewers and makes the audience feel as if they are talking to them.

PROFESSIONAL VIEWPOINT

'The industry is so vibrant and exciting, it's unpredictable and forever changing. If you can hack the pace and emotional rollercoaster that comes with being a presenter at times, then welcome to the gang! It's the best job in the world, and I'm grateful every day.'
Anna Williamson, TV presenter

➔

For many types of programme, presenters need the right look. This man would be perfect for a children's TV show, but totally wrong for a current-affairs programme.

Social media strategist

Are you a Tweeter and do you keep in touch with friends using Facebook? Social media strategists help companies use social media such as Twitter, Pinterest and Facebook to generate online interest about them or their products with people like you! For companies, this is a more focused way of finding possible customers than just advertising their products on their own website.

↑ A social media strategist might help a dentist put up YouTube clips of satisfied patients to encourage new patients to sign up to their practice!

Job description

Social media strategists:

- work with clients to explore and identify ways to integrate social media into business strategies and marketing campaigns
- research the company to identify platforms that its potential customers are likely to use
- suggest how a company should use that platform, such as blogs or video clips
- explain how companies should communicate with customers
- monitor and measure how a strategy or post is working and adapt their strategies accordingly
- monitor competitors and trends in use of social media.

What skills do I need?

One of the main skills that a social media strategist needs is a real interest in social media. They should know how to use them and how to engage with the online community. They need good communication skills, for example, to write creative blog posts. They also need to be good at analysing statistics and be able to work with other departments in a company, including marketing and sales.

Social media strategists work out the types of social media that a company's potential customers are likely to use. For example, a computer games company may target men aged 18 to 35, who might often visit specialist games forums and discussion boards. Then the strategist posts features such as tweets, photos, blogs and video clips about the games that people might follow. Strategists also start comment threads to generate feedback, which they can respond to.

↓ Social media strategists help companies use the power of social media to communicate with a wide target audience in an instant.

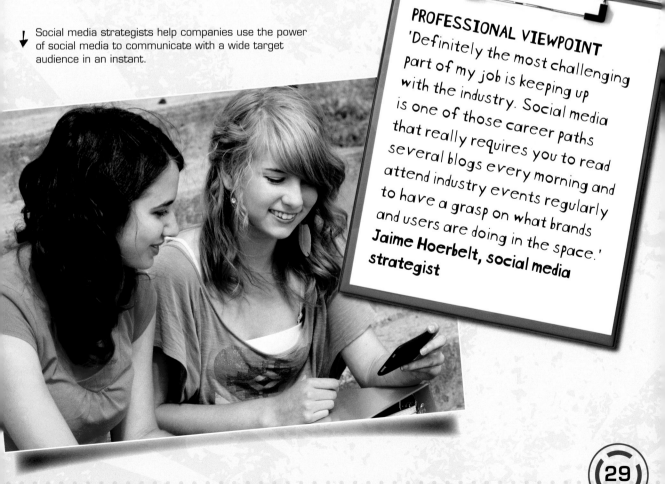

PROFESSIONAL VIEWPOINT

'Definitely the most challenging part of my job is keeping up with the industry. Social media is one of those career paths that really requires you to read several blogs every morning and attend industry events regularly to have a grasp on what brands and users are doing in the space.' **Jaime Hoerbelt, social media strategist**

Glossary

account team group of people that work together for a particular client

archives stores of things like documents, pictures, films and files from the past

autocue device that displays words for people to read

commission employ someone to make something such as a film or advert

copyright when someone owns the copyright on something like a book or film, it cannot be copied without their permission

edit improve, correct or choose what to leave in and what to cut out of something like a book or a film

floor manager person who works in the TV studio, communicating information from the director to the crew on the studio floor and back to the director again

forums Internet message boards

freelance someone who works freelance is self-employed. They are not employed by a particular organisation, but work for several different ones.

genre style or type; crime fiction is a genre of literature

layout way in which text or pictures are set out on a page

logistics practical organisation needed to make a plan work, such as getting equipment to a film set

media main ways in which people receive information and entertainment, such as television, Internet, radio, newspapers and magazines

negotiation discussion to work out a solution to a problem that suits all sides involved

news anchor presents news in broadcast programmes

pitch short summary of an idea, such as the description of a potential story that a writer sends to an editor

platforms different types of media, such as Twitter, YouTube or Facebook, where information, views and advertising can be communicated to a ready-made audience

postgraduate course or study that a student does after their first degree

press cutting excerpt cut from a newspaper or magazine

press release official statement issued to newspapers giving information on a particular matter, such as news about a new play at a theatre

proofread read a piece of text and mark any errors for correction

salient most noticeable or important

social media media designed for social interaction, such as a website that lets you comment on something, or Facebook, which lets you communicate with friends

stills single shots from a film or TV programme, which look like photos

strategist person who makes plans to help a company achieve a particular purpose

unbiased fair and not influenced by your own or other people's opinions

verbal to do with words

Further information

There are many different media jobs out there, in addition to the jobs described in this book. To find out about other work you can do in the media world, read other books and check out websites for ideas. Some suggestions are listed here on this page. It is also really useful to talk to careers advisers at school or college, and to attend careers and college or university fairs to find out about the options available. The earlier you check out the jobs that appeal to you and what will help you get them, the sooner you will be able to start doing the activities – such as editing a school newspaper – that will help you.

Books

Choosing Your A Levels: and other academic options, Cerys Evans, Trotman, 2012

Reading and Writing (Jobs If You Like…), Charlotte Guillain, Heinemann Educational Books, 2012

I'm Good at English: What Job Can I Get? Richard Spilsbury, Wayland, 2011

Advertising and Marketing (Ferguson's Careers in Focus), Facts On File, 2009

Journalist (Cool Careers) William David Thomas, Gareth Stevens Publishing, 2009

Going Live in 3, 2, 1: Have You Got What It Takes to Be a TV Producer? (On the Job), Celia Stewart & Lisa Thompson, Compass Point Books, 2009

Websites

www.prospects.ac.uk/options_media_studies_your_skills.htm
This website is a useful guide to your job options. It is aimed at media studies graduates and it gives a clear idea of what routes to take for many media careers. There is also a list of resources and contacts on this site.

www.careers.guardian.co.uk/media-jobs
This newspaper website has lots of articles about careers in media, and advice on media-related topics such as how to build a successful blog.

www.bbc.co.uk/careers/what-we-do
This BBC website has information about what jobs and types of careers are available in TV.

www.creativeskillset.org/careers
This website has information about a variety of industries and career paths that might interest you, under headings such as Film, Interactive Media and Publishing.

www.targetjobs.co.uk/career-sectors/media-journalism-and-publishing
This website offers advice about courses and experience required for careers in journalism and publishing.

Index

advertising 5, 8, 9, 19
advertising account executives 14–15
advertising agency 14, 15
assistant film editors 24–25
audiences 13, 23, 26

blogs 28, 29
broadcast journalists 16–17

charities 18, 19
clients 14, 15
computer games 21, 29
copywriters 15
creative team 15

degrees 6, 9, 11, 13, 17, 18, 23, 27
documentaries 6, 7

English 6
exhibitions 18, 19

Facebook 9, 28
film crew 10, 12, 13
film editing 24, 25
films 4, 5, 10, 11, 12, 13, 20, 21, 24, 25

government departments 19

illustrators 15
information officers 18–19
Internet 4, 17
interviews 16, 17
IT skills 18, 25

journalism 6, 16–17

locations 6, 7, 10, 12

magazine features editors 22–23
magazines 22, 23
media interviews 19
media planners 8–9
media studies 6
mobiles 5
museums 19

photographers 15, 22
Pinterest 28
press conferences 19
press officers 18–19
programme researchers 6–7
publishing 5

radio 5, 6, 11
radio presenters 16
research 6–7, 8, 9
runners 10–11

screenwriters 20-21
scripts 7
soap operas 20
social media 5, 9, 28, 29
social media strategists 28–29

technology 4, 5
theatre 19
TV 4, 5, 6, 10, 11, 12, 16, 17, 19, 20, 21
TV presenters 26–27
TV producer-directors 12–13
Twitter 9, 28

websites 28, 31
work experience 11, 13, 15, 17, 25

I'M GOOD AT...

Contents of all the titles in the series:

I'M GOOD AT ART
978 0 7502 7768 6
The world of art
Illustrator
Art conservator
Fashion designer
Art teacher
Photographer
Graphic designer
Arts development officer
Curator
Advertising art director
Architect
Art therapist
Artist

I'M GOOD AT MEDIA
978 0 7502 7767 9
The world of media
Programme researcher
Media planner
Runner
TV producer-director
Advertising account executive
Broadcast journalist
Information officer
Screenwriter
Magazine features editor
Assistant film editor
TV presenter
Social-media strategist

I'M GOOD AT GEOGRAPHY
978 0 7502 7766 2
The world of geography
Tourism officer
Park ranger
Environmental consultant
Geologist
Meteorologist
International aid worker
Transport planner
Travel writer
Cartographer

Geographical information
    systems officer
Town planner
Geography teacher

I'M GOOD AT HISTORY
978 0 7502 7769 3
The world of history
Heritage manager
Information officer
Museum conservator
Academic librarian
Archaeologist
Politician's assistant
Trade union researcher
Lawyer
History teacher
Charity fundraiser
Historic buildings inspector
Historical writer

I'M GOOD AT ENGLISH
978 0 7502 7096 0
The world of English
Advertising copywriter
Broadcasting researcher
Theatre director
Newspaper journalist
Archivist
Public relations officer
Librarian
Legal clerk
Author
Editor
Bookseller
English teacher

I'M GOOD AT ICT
978 0 7502 7098 4
The world of ICT
Web designer
Recording engineer

Database administrator
Graphic designer
Telecommunications engineer
Software developer
IT technical sales specialist
Games designer
IT services worker
Computer hardware engineer
Animator
IT trainer

I'M GOOD AT MATHS
978 0 7502 7097 7
The world of maths
Banker
Cryptographer
Accountant
Economist
Finance officer
Computer programmer
Actuary
Medical statistician
Government research analyst
Engineer
Business analyst
Maths teacher

I'M GOOD AT SCIENCE
978 0 7502 7099 1
The world of science
Doctor
Astronomer
Biochemist
Nurse
Geologist
Vet
Meteorologist
Physiotherapist
Dentist
Biologist
Dietitian
Forensic scientist

WAYLAND